ACTIONBOOK

FINISH
YOUR RACE

THIS ACTIONBOOK BELONGS TO:

Name: _____

Address: _____

Telephone: _____

Cell: _____

Email: _____

Support Information:
Don@DonArmstrongLive.com
www.DonArmstrongLive.com

ACTIONBOOK

FINISH
YOUR RACE

Empower
Your
Life with
Strategies
from a
**Cancer
Survivor**

DON ARMSTRONG

Table of Contents

Introduction

In September 2005 I was diagnosed with acute myeloid leukemia (AML), a blood cancer that threatened to end my life. Early in my journey (race), I learned that fewer than 25 - 30 percent of those diagnosed with AML survive beyond five years. I endured five rounds of chemo in eight months, culminating in a successful stem cell transplant on May 12, 2006. This was my new "birthday" and a second chance at life. On that day, I became a "survivor".

Battling cancer was an eye opener and taught me a great deal about myself and life in general. My journey (race) was filled with uncertainty and challenges on a day by day basis. This race was also filled with victories which lead to an understanding of life lessons and valuable life strategies that changed almost every aspect of my life. I discovered that adversity affects all of us, but it doesn't define us — the way we react to adversity determines and changes the outcome.

The *Finish YOUR Race* ActionBook was written to share the extraordinary lessons and strategies learned while my life was on the line. The ActionBook will take you on a journey to discover your race, while adding joy and fulfillment to your life. The ultimate goal is to add value to your life and enhance the legacy you leave for your family and friends.

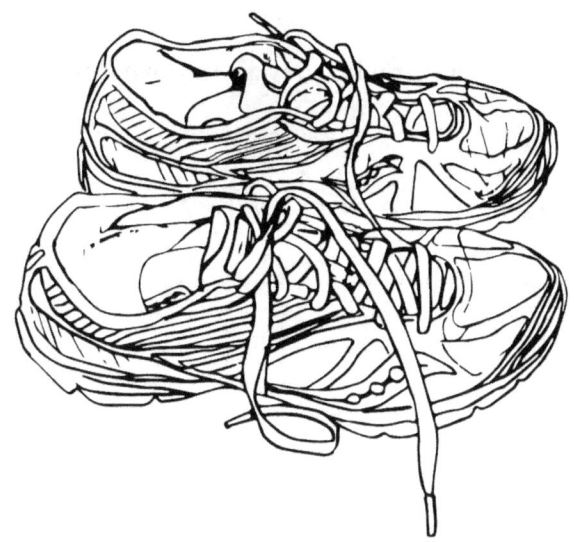

My Story, Your Story, We All Have a Story

"Everyone is necessarily the hero of his own life story."

—John Barth

Everyone has their own story that is uniquely yours. You own it! Your story comes from the circumstances and experiences of your life. More often than not, you may be reluctant to share or tell your story because there's no real need or necessity to share the personal details of your life. Plus, there's a certain amount of vulnerability to sharing your story. This vulnerability may keep us from telling others our story to keep us safe. So, why even explore your story much less share it? Great question! When you understand your story, or another person's story, it sheds light on the life events which made that person who they are today. As a result, it's important you know and better understand yourself through your story.

Many of your stories have defining moments that signaled a significant change in the direction of your life; sometimes negative & sometimes positive. For me, it was my diagnosis of leukemia. These defining moments can be the missing piece in understanding who you are and may help to explain your connection or lack of connection to others in your life.

Understanding your story will help you move forward in your life in a positive, more productive way. Understanding someone else's story will make you aware of the challenges, adversity and live events that have molded and shaped the person they are today. This understanding will help you be a better friend,

SEE PAGES 1-14

1

mentor and supporter and more accepting of who they are and what makes them tick. Let's get started by answering some probing questions.

Are you predominantly a thinker or a doer? Why?

_____

_____

_____

_____

Give 3 reasons you made this assessment.

1. _____

_____

2. _____

_____

3. _____

_____

What (for you) are the best outcomes of thinking combined with doing?

_____

_____

_____

My Race Against Leukemia:

I Am a Survivor

"We shall draw from the heart of suffering itself the means of inspiration and survival."

—Winston Churchill

My challenge was Leukemia. Everyone has their own unique challenge(s).

There are many different areas of one's life: spiritual, relationships, professional/career, recreation, health & fitness, finance, volunteerism, and philanthropy.

From the above list, in which areas do you feel the most challenged?

_____

_____

_____

_____

_____

_____

SEE PAGES 15-26

Why?

_____

_____

_____

_____

_____

_____

If you were to choose one area to focus on for improvement which would it be? Give one reason to achieve the area you selected.

_____

_____

_____

_____

_____

_____

Choose To Be a Survivor

"You can be a victim of cancer, or a survivor of cancer. It's a mindset."

—Dave Pelzer

Are you a VICTIM or a SURVIVOR? Why?

_____

_____

_____

_____

_____

What circumstance(s) have you survived?

_____

_____

_____

_____

_____

SEE PAGES 27–38

Why do you believe you survived these circumstances?

_____

_____

_____

_____

_____

Which current issue do you choose to overcome?

_____

_____

_____

_____

_____

_____

Why?

_____

_____

_____

_____

_____

How?

_____

_____

_____

_____

_____

Identify Your Race

"I have fought the good fight, I have finished the race, I have kept the faith."

—2 Timothy 4:7

Your race is the real deal, something you live every single day. It's the reason you get up every day—your **Why**.

Your **Why** may be about money, personal satisfaction, recognition, achievement, giving, relationships, survival, or something else. It's likely a combination of all these things. Everyone has a **Why**. Have you ever sat down to consider yours, or, even better, have you written it down? Let's get started:

Have you thought about your Why recently? What is your Why? Explain your thoughts.

_____

_____

_____

_____

_____

SEE PAGES 39-56

Your Why is connected to a Who. In other words, Who you are running your race for; yourself, your family, others, etc. Explain your Who!

_____

_____

_____

_____

_____

Does your Who know & understand your Why? Have you discussed with your Who? Explain your thoughts.

_____

_____

_____

_____

_____

Finding your race involves self-discovery. Here's a few questions to get you started:

What do you hope to accomplish in your life?

_____

_____

_____

_____

Are you where you dreamed you'd be when you were a kid or young adult? Explain

_____

_____

_____

_____

Describe your dream!

_____

_____

_____

_____

_____

How is today's reality different from your earlier dreams and aspirations?

_____

_____

_____

_____

_____

What do you dream about accomplishing at this time in your life? Explain in detail.

_____

_____

_____

_____

_____

What captivated your young mind when thinking about
the future? Hint: maybe a person, place or thing?

_____

_____

_____

_____

_____

_____

As a young person, what did you want to accomplish in your life?

_____

_____

_____

_____

_____

At this time in your life, do you feel trapped in a comfort zone
that you don't believe you can escape? Explain

_____

_____

_____

_____

_____

If so, what is your comfort zone? Give it a name & write about it.

_____

_____

_____

_____

What do you dream about accomplishing in your future?

_____

_____

_____

_____

What motivates you on a day by day basis? Money, satisfaction, recognition, achievement, philanthropy, relationships, getting by, or something else? Explore & write about each of the motivations selected from above.

_____

_____

_____

_____

_____

What fears, distractions, obligations, or other personal limitations do you feel are holding you back?

_____

_____

_____

_____

_____

Why?

_____

_____

_____

_____

How?

_____

_____

_____

_____

It's not about you. Contribution of time/money & helping others is one way to turn everything around. Consider moving your focus from you to looking outside yourself. What can you do to help others?

_____

_____

_____

_____

_____

Now that you've answered some questions about yourself in order to know yourself better, what is your race(s) during this time of your life?

_____

_____

_____

_____

_____

Why do you consider this to be your race(s) at this time?

_____

_____

_____

_____

_____

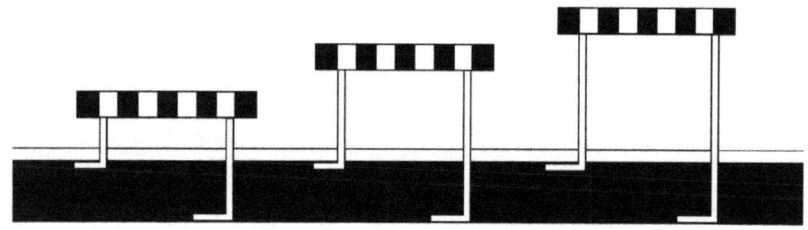

Adversity Happens:

Jumping Over Hurdles

"It's not what happens to you, but how you react to it that matters."

—Epictetus

There are four ways to react to adversity. You can:

1. Allow it to define you,
2. Allow it to consume and ultimately destroy you,
3. Allow it to strengthen you, or
4. Allow it to be an opportunity for change and growth.

Though it may not feel like it sometimes, hear me clearly: the choice is ***yours***.

SEE PAGES 57-71

We all have a pattern we follow in reaction to adversity. Which one of the above reactions describes your reaction? Why? Describe your reaction in detail.

_____

_____

_____

_____

_____

_____

_____

Is this how you prefer to respond or would you like to make a change in your response in the future?

_____

_____

_____

_____

_____

How would you change your response?

_____

_____

_____

_____

_____

Here are some strategies that have worked for me when a challenge arises:

- Stay calm. When in doubt, take a deep breath.
- Remain grounded. Avoid jumping to a worst-case scenario or overreacting.
- Trust yourself and your instincts. You're stronger than you think.
- React with clear and rational thinking by defining your options and thinking through solutions.
- Find ways to maintain a sense of normalcy, even if it's as simple as committing to brush your teeth each morning and evening. Or, in my situation, declining to wear a hospital gown.
- Focus and do your best to avoid being swept up by anxiety or fear.
- Believe in yourself and trust in your faith for courage and strength.
- Seek support from family, friends, a mentor, a professional counselor, or a minister.
- Develop an achievable game plan and have a backup plan in the event that your primary approach doesn't give the results you need.
- Sleep on it. The older I've gotten, the more I understand that it's better to think before you react to just about anything. Time will assist you in clarifying your plan.
- Understand that no matter what, nothing and no one can prevent you from choosing how to react to a challenge.
- Never, ever quit—adversity is your call to action. So take action. Remember, even not taking action is a decision.

Now that you've read some possible strategies (above) and an unexpected misfortune comes crashing into your world, which of these options might work for you? Feel free to list as many as you think would be appropriate for you:

_____

_____

_____

_____

_____

_____

_____

Which of the above strategies seems most appropriate to you for your personality type? List the reason (s) why!

_____

_____

_____

_____

_____

_____

_____

Attitude Is Everything:

Develop a Winning Attitude

"Nothing can stop the man with the right mental attitude from achieving his goal."

—Thomas Jefferson

Give some thought to where your attitude comes from.

Attitudes are contagious. Sleep with dogs that have fleas and you will have fleas.

What does your attitude convey to others? Describe it? If your attitude is a winning attitude to others, describe it

_____

_____

_____

_____

_____

_____

SEE PAGES 73-88

What type of person does your attitude attract? Give an example of someone like that in your life.

_____

_____

_____

_____

_____

_____

_____

When the going gets tough—let's say you've recently lost your job—how do _you_ turn those nagging, negative voices into supportive self-talk?

_____

_____

_____

_____

_____

_____

_____

Here's what works for me:

1. Take a deep breath, hit the pause button, and remember your past successes. All is not lost. You're not a failure. Just because you lost your job doesn't mean you won't get another one.

2. Understand that you are resilient. You're stronger than you think. You _can_ find another job. This is not the end of the world. The sun really will come up tomorrow. This, too, shall pass.

3. Don't be afraid to turn to the people around you for help. You can and should have a support system, and it's okay to ask for support now. Moreover, it's essential to ask for support.

CHANGE YOUR ATTITUDE, CHANGE YOUR LIFE. The bottom line: You can change your attitude and, in the process, you can change your life.

Are there changes you would like to make *now*? Which one(s) seem productive for you? Why?

_____

_____

_____

_____

_____

_____

_____

Which one(s) seem productive for you and why?

_____

_____

_____

_____

_____

_____

_____

Who can you turn to for help and support?

_____

_____

_____

_____

_____

_____

_____

Why would you choose this person or person(s)?

_____

_____

_____

_____

_____

_____

_____

Find Balance

"Balance is not something you find, it's something you create."

—Jana Kingsford

Keep in mind that we are all really good at justifying what we do and how we use our time. It's human nature to do so, to the point where we don't even consider the potential negative consequences of our actions. I was exceptionally adept at justifying my actions. For example, I had to work seven days a week because my job required my constant attention. One of the lessons I've learned in the past ten years—and *this* is important—is that we do, for the most part, exactly what we want to do, when we want to, and we don't take time to think about or even explain our actions.

You may ask, when is **my** balancing act **unbalanced**?

- ◆ You're up early in the morning; it's dark outside. You get ready for work and off you go. You work all day and come home when it's dark outside. You've been so busy, you really don't have a grasp of what happened at work, and you have even less knowledge of what's going on at home. You haven't seen your kids (awake) for days and probably missed their ball games, dance recitals, etc.
- ◆ You spend your day taking your children from one activity to the other. You have no time to enjoy what they are doing because you're in the taxi business for your family. You may even forget who you are picking up and where they are to go.

SEE PAGES 89-104

- You don't have time to take care of daily living activities (paying bills, grocery shopping, seeing family and friends, etc.) because you are "too busy!"
- You are so busy taking care of the household that you have no time to take care of you. You do nothing for you, don't exercise, don't eat right, don't read, you don't relax, etc.
- You spend hours on some form of electronic device (too many to mention) when you're home, ignoring family and friends, etc.
- You ignore vacations and use the excuse that you "have to work."
- Here's a big one: Your relationships start to fall apart because you are not dedicating enough time to nurturing them.

Does anything on the previous page seem true for you?
Which ones from the list fit for you? Why?

_____

_____

_____

_____

_____

_____

_____

_____

Four areas of life balance can serve as your starting point in your discovery process:

- Spiritual (God)
- Relationships (Family, Friends, and Acquaintances)
- Professional (Work)
- Recreational (Hobbies, Sports, and Fun)

This list is by no means all-inclusive. Your priorities might also include community leadership, volunteer work, or fitness—you fill in the blanks!

Which of these areas have a place in your "life balance"?

_____
_____
_____
_____
_____
_____

What other areas of live balance are significant to you?

_____
_____
_____
_____
_____
_____

Now that you've considered "life balance" areas; what are _your_ primary areas of life balance? Why?

_____
_____
_____
_____
_____
_____

So far, we have only thought through our life balance. Complete the Life Balance Chart on the following page to see how you currently use your time & energy on a daily basis. Work through the chart every day for one week. At the end of one week, you should have a good idea about your current priorities. You may be surprised at the results!

Let's discover your current Life Balance.

Life Balance Chart

	Sunday	Monday	Tuesday	Wednesday	Thursday	Friday	Saturday
6:00/7:00 am							
7:00/8:00 am							
8:00/9:00 am							
9:00/10:00 am							
10:00/11:00 am							
11:00/12:00 am/pm							
12:00/1:00 pm							
1:00/2:00 pm							
2:00/3:00 pm							
3:00/4:00 pm							
4:00/5:00 pm							
5:00/6:00 pm							
6:00/7:00 pm							
7:00/8:00 pm							
8:00/9:00 pm							
9:00/10:00 pm							
10:00/11:00 pm							
11:00/12:00 pm/am							

Life Balance Category Suggestions

- Work • Commuting - to & from work
- Carpooling - driving kids to & from activities
- Community volunteering • Church and/or associated activities
- Exercise/Fitness - working out in the gym, running, cycling, swimming, etc. • Hobbies - Reading, playing, etc.
- Meal prep & eating • Household chores laundry, dishes, cleaning, yard work, etc.
- Television/Computer - FaceBook, video games, Google searches, email, internet activities, etc.
- Paying bills

Go to **DonArmstrongLive.com** for a full size usable version of this chart

After you've completed the chart for one week, what did you find?

_____

_____

_____

_____

_____

Life balance and, ultimately, harmony _can_ exist in your life. Self-evaluation is a great starting point, and continued reevaluation is an ongoing and necessary process. Finding balance is a four-step process:

◆ First and foremost, _you must make life balance a priority._

◆ Second, you need to _identify_ what matters most to you by collecting information about how you currently spend your time.

◆ Third, you need to _evaluate_ this information to determine whether you are spending your time in a way that is in harmony with what you value most.

◆ Finally, if you find that your life is out of balance, you can find ways to _improve_ your connection with life balance.

Now do you have a better idea of which aspects of your life aren't being attended to and nurtured?

_____

_____

_____

_____

What surprised you about the results of the Life Balance Chart?

_____

_____

_____

_____

What will you change and how will you change it?

_____

_____

_____

_____

_____

This process was revealing to me. The easiest way to move toward a more balanced life is to first and foremost eliminate activities that zap your time and energy yet don't contribute to your quality of life, such as mindless Internet, email, and television viewing, among other things. Identify the areas that drain your time and eliminate them from your life, little by little or all at once. Just like you have the power to choose your attitude, you have the power to choose how you spend your time. This was huge for me, as I worked to improve balance in my life.

What areas did you identify that zap your time & energy?

_____

_____

_____

_____

_____

_____

_____

Understand Expectations for Yourself and Others

"A wonderful gift may not be wrapped as you expect."

—Jonathan Lockwood Huie

Expectations are derived from your life experiences starting the day you are born and affect every area of your life. They are powerful enough to influence your perception of an outcome both good and not so good. Expectations play an important role in how you encounter life and can have a profound impact on your business and personal life.

Review your expectations periodically to make sure they still hold true for you. Expectations will more than likely change and evolve over time, so don't be afraid to adjust your expectations often and when appropriate. When a conflict results from unfulfilled expectations, stop and think before reacting. Be realistic when expectations, either your own or someone else's, are not met. Understand that expectations are at times influenced by circumstances that are out of your control, and try to adjust accordingly.

Take time to sit down and think about your expectations for various aspects of your life including college, work, marriage, family, parenthood, friendships, health, recreation, fitness, hobbies, and retirement. Once you've thought about these expectations, write down what you discover about yourself in as much detail as possible. Use the Expectations Chart on the following page to record your findings.

SEE PAGES 105-122

1. Write down your expectations for each of the areas in the chart.

2. Consider the origins of your expectations.

3. Compare your expectations with the expectations of the important people in your life.

Expectation Chart

	Expectation(s)	Your Expectation	Origin of Expectation	Other's Expectation	Differences	Resolution/ Understanding
College						
Work						
Marriage						
Family						
Parenthood						
Friendships						
Health						
Recreation/Fitness						
Hobbies/Fun						
Retirement						

Go to **DonArmstrongLive.com** for a full size usable version of this chart

Do your expectations reflect what you truly believe?

_____

_____

_____

_____

_____

_____

If so, what do you believe?

_____

_____

_____

_____

_____

_____

_____

Do some of your expectations reflect what others want?

_____

_____

_____

_____

_____

_____

_____

Explain in detail:

_____

_____

_____

_____

_____

_____

_____

Have you discussed your expectations with others?

_____

_____

_____

_____

_____

_____

With whom did you have this discussion? Who are they in your life?

_____

_____

_____

_____

_____

_____

Following the discussion, how did your expectations differ? Why?

_____

_____

_____

_____

_____

_____

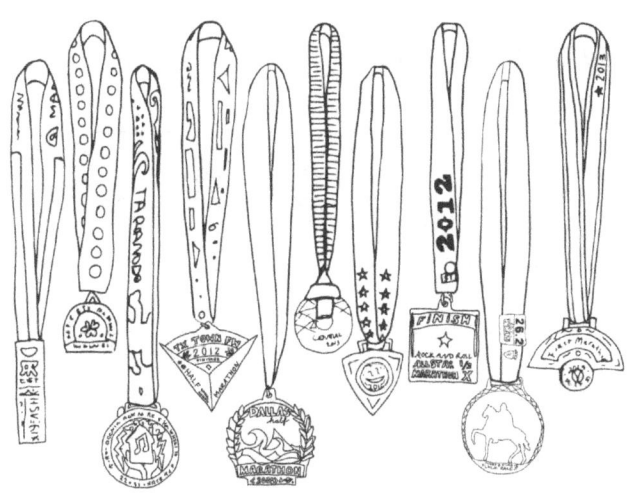

Combine Purpose With Passion

"Purpose is the reason you journey. Passion is the fire that lights your way."

—Author Unknown

Why am I here?
Where am I going?
What's important to me?
How am I making a difference?

Think about your legacy. When you leave this earth no one will remember how much money you made, the size of your house, which car you drove, or the vacations you took. They will, however, remember the depth of how you impacted their lives.

Find a quiet space and let your mind settle. You might take five or ten minutes to sit in silence, breathe deeply, or meditate. The following exercise may take some time, and if you need to let these questions simmer and come back to them later, that's okay.

Let's start the process of finding your purpose. Here are a series of questions to help you figure it out.

Is there something you've always dreamed of doing in your life? Is there a dream from your past (locked in your heart and head) that you've all but forgotten? Is there something you want to do within your lifetime? Something you are not currently doing? Focus on the dream!

SEE PAGES 123–135

Write it down with clarity & explanation!

_____

_____

_____

_____

_____

What did you love doing as a child? Playing outside? Spending time with playmates? Reading books? Drawing? Games?

_____

_____

_____

_____

_____

List at least 3-5 ideas or thoughts that are true for you!

_____

_____

_____

_____

_____

_____

_____

_____

_____

If you had all the money you needed, what would you do to contribute to the world?

_____

_____

_____

_____

_____

_____

What would you do for absolutely no pay?

_____

_____

_____

_____

_____

_____

_____

What do you absolutely love to do? What gives you joy and excitement? What would you happily devote hours doing if you had all the time in the world? Explain in detail:

_____

_____

_____

_____

_____

_____

What are you good at without even trying? What are your talents and gifts?
What makes you feel terrific about yourself? List at least 3 things!

_____

_____

_____

_____

_____

_____

What do you enjoy talking about with friends, family, and colleagues? What
do you enjoy reading, researching, or studying? What do you Google?

_____

_____

_____

_____

_____

_____

_____

When was the last time you felt excited? Exhilarated?
What was the source of this feeling?

_____

_____

_____

_____

_____

Were you excited because of what you were doing? Explain:

_____

_____

_____

_____

_____

_____

_____

What do you hope to do with your life?

_____

_____

_____

_____

_____

_____

_____

What is the one accomplishment you would like to
achieve before the end of your life?

_____

_____

_____

_____

_____

_____

What would you regret not doing, being, or having in your life?

_____
_____
_____
_____
_____
_____

What "cause" motivates you to volunteer? What would you like to do to improve your corner of the world?

_____
_____
_____
_____
_____
_____

Will your "cause" make a difference in your life or, more importantly, someone else's life? Or, both?

_____
_____
_____
_____
_____
_____

What would your friends and family say you're good at doing? What would they say are your dreams and hopes? Is there something others ask you to help them with on a frequent basis? Take time to ask your friends for feedback.

_____

_____

_____

_____

_____

_____

Your answers to the above questions are just the beginning of knowing and understanding yourself and your race in life. Hopefully, the answers to these questions will bring you closer to discovering your purpose. Hopefully this exercise got some ideas flowing. If your purpose didn't come to you instantly, don't worry. Give it time, and keep revisiting these questions.

Passion is an intense emotion! In fact, it may be your most important asset. I would call it your secret sauce, like McDonald's has for the Big Mac. **Passion is an energy force and an energy source. Passion supports your purpose.**

What is your passion?

_____

_____

_____

_____

_____

_____

Purpose is the marriage of passion and action. It's the fuel that moves you forward every single day. It can act as your key to success and help get you through difficult times. A true and real passion (this is an action word) is natural and tireless. You can't fake real passion. It's something you feel and know.

Discover Your Direction: Set Goals

"Setting goals is the first step in turning the invisible into the visible."

—Tony Robbins

Goal-setting is a process. Look for reasons to succeed (and you will!), not reasons you can't succeed.

GOAL-SETTING STEP 1: SET SPECIFIC GOALS – PAGE 148

Set one specific goal:

_____

_____

_____

_____

_____

_____

_____

SEE PAGES 137-153

GOAL-SETTING STEP 2: SELECT A DEADLINE
FOR GOAL COMPLETION –PAGE 150

Select a deadline for that goal:

_____

_____

_____

_____

_____

_____

_____

_____

GOAL-SETTING STEP 3: WRITE DOWN YOUR GOAL – PAGE 150

Write your goal in a way that is very specific. "I am going to lose weight",
is not a specific goal. A better way to state a weight-loss goal would
be say, "I want to lose 20 pounds during the next 10 months."

_____

_____

_____

_____

_____

_____

_____

_____

_____

GOAL-SETTING STEP 4: DEVELOP A PLAN AND COMMIT TO IT – PAGE 151

Write down clear steps to meet your goal.

_____

_____

_____

_____

_____

_____

_____

_____

GOAL-SETTING STEP 5: REVIEW YOUR GOAL(S) EVERY DAY – PAGE 152

Setting specific, written goals, combined with a clearly defined plan to achieve success is paramount; however, you absolutely must review your goals on a regular basis.

Read or write your goals twice a day, in the morning to motivate you, and in the evening to renew your focus.

The Power of Action

"The distance between dreams and reality is called action."

—Author Unknown

Action is defined as "the process or state of acting or of being active; something done or performed; act; deed." **Applying action leads to results.** Action brings a goal to fruition, leads to solutions for a problem, and turns adversity around, resulting in more predictable successes. With action, everything you think, believe, and hope for can and will be accomplished. You must be willing to take action to move forward. Once again, it's up to you!

Action = Change = Success

My battle with cancer taught me that we often surrender to distractions. I had plenty of distractions during my journey that could have easily derailed my road to recovery.

Complex distractions, on the other hand, are generally self-induced and originate in our minds. These distractions have a tendency to result in self-sabotage and often keep us from succeeding. There is a long list of these distractions: fear, including fear of failure, fear of success, fear of the unknown, fear of change, and fear of rejection. Additional complex distractions include doubt, worry, uncertainty, insecurity, memories, experiences, and procrastination. Complex distractions become excuses and can ultimately take control of our ability or inability to be successful. **In other words, complex distractions can limit our beliefs, sabotage progress and, ultimately, our future.**

SEE PAGES 155-171

List the distractions you have allowed to take your
focus away from achieving your goals:

_____

_____

_____

_____

_____

_____

Failure is never final.

You're never a failure until you quit,

and it's always too soon to quit.

You don't determine a person's greatness by his talent,

his wealth, or his education.

You determine a person's greatness

by what it takes to discourage him."

—Rick Warren

In an effort to free yourself from distractions:

• Create an environment that allows you to focus. Where
  (or what) is your most productive environment?

_____

_____

_____

_____

_____

- Take on one task or project at a time. Prioritize your tasks.

- Set aside a specific amount of time to focus on a task,
  and make your best effort to avoid distractions.

- Focus on what you are striving to achieve, NOT the distractions
  (excuses) that keep you from being successful.

- When you feel frustrated or discouraged about your lack of progress
  toward a goal, remember your Why to move forward again.

Re-write your Why in a few very precise words:

_____

_____

_____

_____

_____

_____

Only by making things happen can you realize change. Action is the way to change your situation and impact your outcome for the better!

Finish YOUR Race

"Each day is a new beginning."

—Michael Duff Newton

My journey with leukemia revealed to me so many important facets of life which I never previously considered. Here's a recap of the themes I have embraced:

- **Adversity** affects all of us at one time or another. It's not the adversity itself, but how we react to it that can define and change the direction and outcome of our lives.

- **Attitude** is a game changer. By changing your attitude, you can change your life and determine the course of your future.

- **Balance** is an important concept to be aware of, as it affects so many areas of our lives: work, play, relationships, and more. However, don't obsess about life balance. Instead, be conscious of how life balance affects yourself and others. Learn to be flexible in applying this concept to your daily life.

- **Expectations** are derived from your life experiences, from the day you were born, and affect every area of your life. Expectations are powerful enough to influence your perception of an outcome, both good and not so good.

SEE PAGES 173–178

- **Purpose** is a powerful motivator in your life, providing meaning and direction to every waking hour of the day. Purpose and passion are not the same, yet they are inseparable. Purpose is your reason and passion is the energy which powers the way.

- **Goal Setting** can make a difference in your life. It is not New Year's resolutions, but a process that works and leads to your success.

- **Action** is the catalyst that can make an idea a reality, the relentless effort that can solve a problem, and the ingredient that can bring a goal to fruition. Distractions, of all types, can and do slow or stop your actions. Focus combined with action can help you overcome distractions and lead to even quicker and more meaningful success.

It's *never* too late to make a difference in yourself and others. With courage, focus, and a positive spirit, you *can* discover, or rediscover, what living your best life means to you. So what are you waiting for? Get out there, get started and *Finish YOUR Race!*

Are you ready to get started? Why?

_____

_____

_____

_____

_____

_____

What is your first step toward completing your goal?

_____

_____

_____

_____

_____

_____

What action(s) do you need to *Finish YOUR Race?*

_____

_____

_____

_____

_____

_____

_____

_____

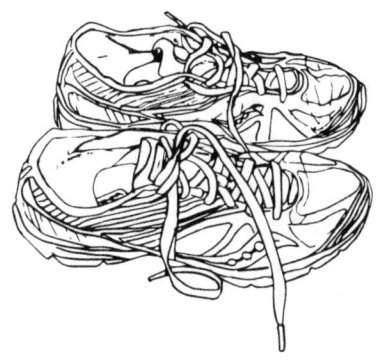

Race Resources

Several organizations were important to me during my race with leukemia. Each of these organizations played a special and vital role in my survival. Collectively, they were the team that got me across the finish line. I am forever grateful for this team and their extraordinary efforts. I would like you to know more about these important nonprofits and hospitals and the roles they may play in a cancer patient's journey. Please take the time to check out these resources on the pages ahead. If you ever need support, you've got a place to call.

fighting blood cancers

The **Leukemia & Lymphoma Society (LLS)** is the world's largest voluntary health agency dedicated to blood cancer. The LLS mission: Cure leukemia, lymphoma, Hodgkin's disease and myeloma, and improve the quality of life of patients and their families. LLS funds lifesaving blood cancer research around the world and provides free information and support services. LLS exists to find cures and ensure access to treatments for blood cancer patients. We are the voice for all blood cancer patients and we work to ensure access to treatments for all blood cancer patients.

www.lls.org

BE THE MATCH®

For people with life-threatening blood cancers—like leukemia and lymphoma—or other diseases, a cure exists. **Be The Match** connects patients with their donor match for a life-saving marrow or umbilical cord blood transplant. Be The Match provides patients and their families one-on-one support, education, and guidance before, during and after transplant You can help save a life as a committed member of the Be The Match Registry®, financial contributor or volunteer. To learn more about the cure, visit BeTheMatch.org or call 1 (800) MARROW-2.

BeTheMatch.org

Carter BloodCare's primary purpose is to make blood transfusions available for hospital patients within its regional service area. The blood center is a not-for-profit, 501(c) 3 organization that recruits blood donors, collects blood from volunteer donors; processes, tests and distributes the blood products to more than 200 medical facilities in more than 55 counties. Headquarters and service areas are located in north, central and east Texas. To make an appointment, call 1-800-DONATE-4 (800-366-2834) or visit www.carterbloodcare.org. The blood program is licensed by the U.S. Food and Drug Administration, accredited by AABB and is a member of America's Blood Centers.

www.carterbloodcare.org

Texas Health
Harris Methodist Hospital®
FORT WORTH

The Klabzuba Cancer Center at Texas Health Harris Methodist Hospital Fort Worth provides quality care throughout the cancer journey. The program's vision of striving for a future without cancer is reflected in its continuum of services: prevention, screening, early detection, treatment planning, surgery, chemotherapy, radiation, rehabilitation, palliative care and more.

The cancer center received the "Outstanding Achievement Award" from the Commission on Cancer (CoC) of the American College of Surgeons for excellence in the key areas of patient care. This demonstrates the high quality care provided to Texas Health Fort Worth patients from diagnosis, through the treatment period, and beyond.

TexasHealth.org/FW-Cancer

BAYLOR
University Medical Center
at Dallas

Baylor Charles A. Sammons
Cancer Center

Part of ✚ BaylorScott&White HEALTH

For nearly four decades, **Baylor Charles A. Sammons Cancer Center**, an integral part of Baylor University Medical Center at Dallas, has provided quality clinical care, advanced technology, and clinical research to patients, along with comprehensive support services and programs for patients and their families. With the opening of a 10-story outpatient treatment facility and integration with Baylor T. Boone Pickens Cancer Hospital, it is now the largest outpatient cancer center in North Texas. Annually, more than 90,000 cancer visits occur at Baylor Sammons Cancer Center, and more than 800 people participate in research trials.

BaylorScottandWhite.com

CPSIA information can be obtained
at www.ICGtesting.com
Printed in the USA
BVHW012250160419
545763BV00012B/217/P